INNER REFLECTIONS

ENGAGEMENT CALENDAR 2015

SELECTIONS FROM THE WRITINGS OF
PARAMAHANSA YOGANANDA

SELF-REALIZATION FELLOWSHIP

FRONT COVER:
Kauai, Hawaii
Photograph by Terry Donnelly
Design by Shawn Freeman

NOTE: *Holidays and other observed dates are included for the United States (U.S.), Canada, United Kingdom (U.K.), Australia, and New Zealand (N.Z.).*
Moon phases, equinoxes, and solstices are based on Pacific Standard Time (UTC – 8 hours).

Printed in Italy
4825-J2932

The scenery of mountains painted on the ever-changing azure canvas of the sky,
the mysterious mechanism of the human body, the rose, the green grass carpet,
the magnanimity of souls, the loftiness of minds,
the depth of love—all these things remind us
of a God who is beautiful and noble.

—Paramahansa Yogananda

THE PHOTOGRAPHS IN THIS CALENDAR are accompanied by selections from the writings of Paramahansa Yogananda, whose timeless and universal teachings have awakened many, of all races, cultures, and creeds, to a deeper awareness of the one reality that sustains and unites us all.

Whether spread over the vast heavens or hidden in the exquisite delicacy of a tiny flower, nature's beauty is always beckoning, inviting us to look behind the outward form and sense the presence of God within.

We hope that the thoughts and images in these pages will bring you inspiration and encouragement in the days and weeks of the coming year.

Kauai, Hawaii   Photograph by Terry Donnelly

When you are calm, you feel the whole universe of happiness rocking gently beneath your consciousness. That happiness is God.

—Paramahansa Yogananda

Sunrise, Rockland, Maine   Photograph by Paul Rezendes

December/January

29
monday

30
tuesday

31
wednesday

New Year's Day
1
thursday

Bank Holiday (U.K.) Day After New Year's Day (N.Z.)
2
friday

December 2014

S	M	T	W	T	F	S
	1	2	3	4	5	6
7	8	9	10	11	12	13
14	15	16	17	18	19	20
21	22	23	24	25	26	27
28	29	30	31			

3
saturday

January

S	M	T	W	T	F	S
				1	2	3
4	5	6	7	8	9	10
11	12	13	14	15	16	17
18	19	20	21	22	23	24
25	26	27	28	29	30	31

Full Moon ○
4
sunday

January

5
monday
Paramahansa Yogananda's Birthday

6
tuesday

7
wednesday

8
thursday

9
friday

10
saturday

11
sunday

JANUARY

S	M	T	W	T	F	S
				1	2	3
4	5	6	7	8	9	10
11	12	13	14	15	16	17
18	19	20	21	22	23	24
25	26	27	28	29	30	31

FEBRUARY

S	M	T	W	T	F	S
1	2	3	4	5	6	7
8	9	10	11	12	13	14
15	16	17	18	19	20	21
22	23	24	25	26	27	28

When in meditation the mind follows the stream of inner consciousness,
the devotee enters the supernal kingdom of God.

—Paramahansa Yogananda

Barometer Mountain, Kodiak, Alaska   Photograph by Marion Owen

Conquer your circumscribed consciousness
and expand your spiritual powers without limit.
You can go as far as you want to go, past all limitations,
and live a supremely victorious existence.

—Paramahansa Yogananda

Wild horses, Camargue, France   Photograph by Gerard Lacz/Animals Animals

January

12
monday

13
tuesday

Last Quarter ◐

14
wednesday

15
thursday

16
friday

JANUARY

S	M	T	W	T	F	S
				1	2	3
4	5	6	7	8	9	10
11	12	13	14	15	16	17
18	19	20	21	22	23	24
25	26	27	28	29	30	31

FEBRUARY

S	M	T	W	T	F	S
1	2	3	4	5	6	7
8	9	10	11	12	13	14
15	16	17	18	19	20	21
22	23	24	25	26	27	28

17
saturday

18
sunday

January

19
monday

Martin Luther King, Jr.'s Birthday (Observed)

20
tuesday

New Moon ●

21
wednesday

22
thursday

23
friday

24
saturday

25
sunday

January

S	M	T	W	T	F	S
				1	2	3
4	5	6	7	8	9	10
11	12	13	14	15	16	17
18	19	20	21	22	23	24
25	26	27	28	29	30	31

February

S	M	T	W	T	F	S
1	2	3	4	5	6	7
8	9	10	11	12	13	14
15	16	17	18	19	20	21
22	23	24	25	26	27	28

The mysterious soul abides forever, changing never....
It loves to live in the grottos of change, ever steadfast and immovable.
It never dreams aught but eternity.

—Paramahansa Yogananda

Slot canyons, Antelope Canyon, Arizona Photograph by CCOphotostockKMN/Prisma/SUPERSTOCK

Peace is the breath of stones, stars, and sages.
Peace is the ambrosial wine of Spirit flowing from the cask of silence.

—Paramahansa Yogananda

Punchbowl Falls, Columbia River Gorge National Scenic Area, Oregon Photograph by Dennis Frates

January/February

26
monday

Australia Day (Australia) First Quarter ◐

27
tuesday

28
wednesday

29
thursday

30
friday

January

S	M	T	W	T	F	S
				1	2	3
4	5	6	7	8	9	10
11	12	13	14	15	16	17
18	19	20	21	22	23	24
25	26	27	28	29	30	31

February

S	M	T	W	T	F	S
1	2	3	4	5	6	7
8	9	10	11	12	13	14
15	16	17	18	19	20	21
22	23	24	25	26	27	28

31
saturday

1
sunday

February

2
monday

3
tuesday

Full Moon ◯

4
wednesday

5
thursday

6
friday

Waitangi Day (N.Z.)

7
saturday

8
sunday

FEBRUARY

S	M	T	W	T	F	S
1	2	3	4	5	6	7
8	9	10	11	12	13	14
15	16	17	18	19	20	21
22	23	24	25	26	27	28

MARCH

S	M	T	W	T	F	S
1	2	3	4	5	6	7
8	9	10	11	12	13	14
15	16	17	18	19	20	21
22	23	24	25	26	27	28
29	30	31				

In the still lake of my soul,
I love to behold Thine unruffled face of stillness.

—Paramahansa Yogananda

Mount Lorette, Alberta, Canada Photograph by Tim Fitzharris

Love is the divine power of attraction in creation that harmonizes, unites, binds together....
Those who live in tune with the attractive force of love
achieve harmony with nature and their fellow beings.

—Paramahansa Yogananda

Red and white bleeding hearts, Oregon   Photograph by Steve Terrill

February

9
monday

10
tuesday

Last Quarter ◑
11
wednesday

Lincoln's Birthday
12
thursday

13
friday

February

S	M	T	W	T	F	S
1	2	3	4	5	6	7
8	9	10	11	12	13	14
15	16	17	18	19	20	21
22	23	24	25	26	27	28

St. Valentine's Day
14
saturday

March

S	M	T	W	T	F	S
1	2	3	4	5	6	7
8	9	10	11	12	13	14
15	16	17	18	19	20	21
22	23	24	25	26	27	28
29	30	31				

15
sunday

February

16
monday
Presidents' Day

17
tuesday

18
wednesday
New Moon ●

19
thursday

20
friday

21
saturday

22
sunday
Washington's Birthday

February

S	M	T	W	T	F	S
1	2	3	4	5	6	7
8	9	10	11	12	13	14
15	16	17	18	19	20	21
22	23	24	25	26	27	28

March

S	M	T	W	T	F	S
1	2	3	4	5	6	7
8	9	10	11	12	13	14
15	16	17	18	19	20	21
22	23	24	25	26	27	28
29	30	31				

Bring into play the almighty power that is within you,
so that on the stage of life you can fulfill your high destined role.

—Paramahansa Yogananda

Oxbow Bend, Grand Teton National Park, Wyoming   Photograph by Russ Burden

Live more simply, so that you can find time to enjoy the little pleasures of life.

—Paramahansa Yogananda

Polar bear family, Manitoba, Canada   Photograph by Daisy Gilardini/Masterfile

February/March

23
monday

24
tuesday

First Quarter ◐
25
wednesday

26
thursday

27
friday

February

S	M	T	W	T	F	S
1	2	3	4	5	6	7
8	9	10	11	12	13	14
15	16	17	18	19	20	21
22	23	24	25	26	27	28

28
saturday

March

S	M	T	W	T	F	S
1	2	3	4	5	6	7
8	9	10	11	12	13	14
15	16	17	18	19	20	21
22	23	24	25	26	27	28
29	30	31				

St. David's Day (Wales)
1
sunday

March

2
monday

3
tuesday

4
wednesday

5
thursday

Full Moon ○

6
friday

7
saturday

Paramahansa Yogananda's Mahasamadhi

8
sunday

Daylight Saving Time begins (U.S. and Canada)

MARCH

S	M	T	W	T	F	S
1	2	3	4	5	6	7
8	9	10	11	12	13	14
15	16	17	18	19	20	21
22	23	24	25	26	27	28
29	30	31				

APRIL

S	M	T	W	T	F	S
			1	2	3	4
5	6	7	8	9	10	11
12	13	14	15	16	17	18
19	20	21	22	23	24	25
26	27	28	29	30		

Perception of the Absolute beyond creation is intimately close through the intermediary of Its reflected Intelligence in creation.

—Paramahansa Yogananda

Crater Lake and Wizard Island, Crater Lake National Park, Oregon   Photograph by Dennis Frates

Develop the individuality that is an expression of His presence within you, which is your true Self.

—Paramahansa Yogananda

Regent bowerbird, Australia   Photograph by Darrell Gulin

March

9
monday

Sri Yukteswar's Mahasamadhi

10
tuesday

11
wednesday

12
thursday

13
friday

Last Quarter ◑

MARCH

S	M	T	W	T	F	S
1	2	3	4	5	6	7
8	9	10	11	12	13	14
15	16	17	18	19	20	21
22	23	24	25	26	27	28
29	30	31				

APRIL

S	M	T	W	T	F	S
			1	2	3	4
5	6	7	8	9	10	11
12	13	14	15	16	17	18
19	20	21	22	23	24	25
26	27	28	29	30		

14
saturday

15
sunday

Mothering Sunday (U.K.)

March

16
monday

17
tuesday
St. Patrick's Day

18
wednesday

19
thursday

20
friday
Vernal Equinox New Moon ●

21
saturday

22
sunday

MARCH

S	M	T	W	T	F	S
1	2	3	4	5	6	7
8	9	10	11	12	13	14
15	16	17	18	19	20	21
22	23	24	25	26	27	28
29	30	31				

APRIL

S	M	T	W	T	F	S
			1	2	3	4
5	6	7	8	9	10	11
12	13	14	15	16	17	18
19	20	21	22	23	24	25
26	27	28	29	30		

No slightest shadow of doubt about the immediacy of God can remain in the mind of the devotee who perceives the whole manifested universe as the Creator's resplendent raiment.

—Paramahansa Yogananda

North Fork Silver Creek, Silver Falls State Park, Oregon   Photograph by Dennis Frates

Be master of yourself, captain of your destiny.
Danger and you were born together, and you are the elder brother,
more dangerous than danger!

—Paramahansa Yogananda

Lion family, Masai Mara, Kenya   Photograph by Steve Bloom/SteveBloom.com

March

23
monday

24
tuesday

25
wednesday

26
thursday

First Quarter ◐

27
friday

March

S	M	T	W	T	F	S
1	2	3	4	5	6	7
8	9	10	11	12	13	14
15	16	17	18	19	20	21
22	23	24	25	26	27	28
29	30	31				

28
saturday

April

S	M	T	W	T	F	S
			1	2	3	4
5	6	7	8	9	10	11
12	13	14	15	16	17	18
19	20	21	22	23	24	25
26	27	28	29	30		

Daylight Saving Time begins (E.U.)

29
sunday

March/April

30
monday

31
tuesday

1
wednesday

2
thursday

3
friday

Good Friday Passover begins

4
saturday

Full Moon ○

5
sunday

Easter Sunday

MARCH

S	M	T	W	T	F	S
1	2	3	4	5	6	7
8	9	10	11	12	13	14
15	16	17	18	19	20	21
22	23	24	25	26	27	28
29	30	31				

APRIL

S	M	T	W	T	F	S
			1	2	3	4
5	6	7	8	9	10	11
12	13	14	15	16	17	18
19	20	21	22	23	24	25
26	27	28	29	30		

*L*ife sleeps in the crude earth, dreams beauty in the flowers,
wakes with power in the animals,
and in man has consciousness of infinite possibilities.

—Paramahansa Yogananda

Crocus, United Kingdom Photograph by Guy Edwardes/Getty Images

In all our harmonious relations we must remember that it is God who is playing hide-and-seek from behind the living hearts.

—Paramahansa Yogananda

Black bear cub, Minnesota   Photograph by Phyllis Burchett

April

6
monday
Easter Monday (Canada, U.K., Australia, N.Z.)

7
tuesday

8
wednesday

9
thursday

10
friday

11
saturday
Last Quarter ◑

12
sunday

April

S	M	T	W	T	F	S
			1	2	3	4
5	6	7	8	9	10	11
12	13	14	15	16	17	18
19	20	21	22	23	24	25
26	27	28	29	30		

May

S	M	T	W	T	F	S
					1	2
3	4	5	6	7	8	9
10	11	12	13	14	15	16
17	18	19	20	21	22	23
24/31	25	26	27	28	29	30

April

13
monday

14
tuesday

15
wednesday

16
thursday

17
friday

18
saturday

New Moon ●

19
sunday

APRIL

S	M	T	W	T	F	S
			1	2	3	4
5	6	7	8	9	10	11
12	13	14	15	16	17	18
19	20	21	22	23	24	25
26	27	28	29	30		

MAY

S	M	T	W	T	F	S
					1	2
3	4	5	6	7	8	9
10	11	12	13	14	15	16
17	18	19	20	21	22	23
24/31	25	26	27	28	29	30

O Master Weaver of Dreams, teach me to loom a cushioning carpet of Self-realization on which all Thy lovers may tread as they travel to the shrine of eternal wakefulness.

—Paramahansa Yogananda

Mount Ranier, Washington   Photograph by Kevin McNeil

Establish in yourself a temple of beauty and peace;
there you will find God, on the altar of your soul.

—Paramahansa Yogananda

Cardinal in dogwood tree, Conyers, Georgia   Photograph by Phyllis Burchett

April

20
monday

21
tuesday

Earth Day
22
wednesday

St. George's Day (England)
23
thursday

24
friday

April

S	M	T	W	T	F	S
			1	2	3	4
5	6	7	8	9	10	11
12	13	14	15	16	17	18
19	20	21	22	23	24	25
26	27	28	29	30		

ANZAC Day (Australia and N.Z.)   First Quarter ◐
25
saturday

May

S	M	T	W	T	F	S
					1	2
3	4	5	6	7	8	9
10	11	12	13	14	15	16
17	18	19	20	21	22	23
24/31	25	26	27	28	29	30

26
sunday

April/May

27
monday

28
tuesday

29
wednesday

30
thursday

1
friday

2
saturday

3
sunday

Full Moon ○

April

S	M	T	W	T	F	S
			1	2	3	4
5	6	7	8	9	10	11
12	13	14	15	16	17	18
19	20	21	22	23	24	25
26	27	28	29	30		

May

S	M	T	W	T	F	S
					1	2
3	4	5	6	7	8	9
10	11	12	13	14	15	16
17	18	19	20	21	22	23
24/31	25	26	27	28	29	30

Spirit manifests Its tenderness in the flowers.

—Paramahansa Yogananda

Delphinium, Venlo, the Netherlands Photograph by Marie Bush

The mother, filled with the tenderness of feminine feeling,
is a symbol of divine compassion.

—Paramahansa Yogananda

Orangutan and baby, Lowry Park Zoo, Tampa, Florida Photograph by Cheryl Arena Molennor

May

4
monday
Early May Bank Holiday (U.K.)

5
tuesday

6
wednesday

7
thursday
National Day of Prayer

8
friday

MAY

S	M	T	W	T	F	S
					1	2
3	4	5	6	7	8	9
10	11	12	13	14	15	16
17	18	19	20	21	22	23
24/31	25	26	27	28	29	30

9
saturday

JUNE

S	M	T	W	T	F	S
	1	2	3	4	5	6
7	8	9	10	11	12	13
14	15	16	17	18	19	20
21	22	23	24	25	26	27
28	29	30				

10
sunday
Sri Yukteswar's Birthday Mother's Day (U.S., Canada, Australia, N.Z.)

May

11
monday
Last Quarter ◑

12
tuesday

13
wednesday

14
thursday

15
friday

16
saturday

17
sunday
New Moon ●

May

S	M	T	W	T	F	S
					1	2
3	4	5	6	7	8	9
10	11	12	13	14	15	16
17	18	19	20	21	22	23
24/31	25	26	27	28	29	30

June

S	M	T	W	T	F	S
	1	2	3	4	5	6
7	8	9	10	11	12	13
14	15	16	17	18	19	20
21	22	23	24	25	26	27
28	29	30				

Right behind space is Intelligence. And right behind you is God.

—Paramahansa Yogananda

Monument Valley, Utah Photograph by Jay O'Brien/Jaynes' Gallery/Danita Delimont Agency

The restless sea, whirlpools of solar systems, eddies of cosmic forces, and icebergs of floating planets are dancing on the breast of eternal motion.

—Paramahansa Yogananda

Ofu Island, American Samoa   Photograph by Jon Cornforth

May

18
monday
Victoria Day (Canada)

19
tuesday

20
wednesday

21
thursday

22
friday

May

S	M	T	W	T	F	S
					1	2
3	4	5	6	7	8	9
10	11	12	13	14	15	16
17	18	19	20	21	22	23
24/31	25	26	27	28	29	30

June

S	M	T	W	T	F	S
	1	2	3	4	5	6
7	8	9	10	11	12	13
14	15	16	17	18	19	20
21	22	23	24	25	26	27
28	29	30				

23
saturday

24
sunday

25
monday

Memorial Day Spring Bank Holiday (U.K.) First Quarter

26
tuesday

27
wednesday

28
thursday

29
friday

30
saturday

31
sunday

MAY

S	M	T	W	T	F	S
					1	2
3	4	5	6	7	8	9
10	11	12	13	14	15	16
17	18	19	20	21	22	23
24/31	25	26	27	28	29	30

JUNE

S	M	T	W	T	F	S
	1	2	3	4	5	6
7	8	9	10	11	12	13
14	15	16	17	18	19	20
21	22	23	24	25	26	27
28	29	30				

Thou art nearer to me than the throbs of my heart;
and I perceive Thee on the farthest horizon of consciousness.

—Paramahansa Yogananda

False Kiva, Canyonlands National Park, Utah Photograph by Steffen & Alexandra/Ardea/Animals Animals

Day by day, as you learn to meditate, a new awakening will come....
The mist of silence and mystery which hangs over everything
will slowly vanish before the dawning light
of your mental and devotional search for God.

—Paramahansa Yogananda

Loch Awe, Argyll, Scotland   Photograph by David Speight/Alamy

June

1
monday
Queen's Birthday (N.Z.)

2
tuesday
Full Moon ◯

3
wednesday

4
thursday

5
friday

6
saturday

7
sunday

June

S	M	T	W	T	F	S
	1	2	3	4	5	6
7	8	9	10	11	12	13
14	15	16	17	18	19	20
21	22	23	24	25	26	27
28	29	30				

July

S	M	T	W	T	F	S
			1	2	3	4
5	6	7	8	9	10	11
12	13	14	15	16	17	18
19	20	21	22	23	24	25
26	27	28	29	30	31	

June

8
monday

Queen's Birthday (Australia)

9
tuesday

Last Quarter ◑

10
wednesday

11
thursday

12
friday

13
saturday

14
sunday

JUNE

S	M	T	W	T	F	S
	1	2	3	4	5	6
7	8	9	10	11	12	13
14	15	16	17	18	19	20
21	22	23	24	25	26	27
28	29	30				

JULY

S	M	T	W	T	F	S
			1	2	3	4
5	6	7	8	9	10	11
12	13	14	15	16	17	18
19	20	21	22	23	24	25
26	27	28	29	30	31	

God is a garden of celestial blossoms and bright thought-flowers.
He is the love that inspires our love-dreams.

—Paramahansa Yogananda

Magnolia stamens, Devon, United Kingdom   Photograph by Guy Edwardes

Awaken that meek yet thunderous divine personality—
strong as the lion, gentle as the dove.

—Paramahansa Yogananda

African lion, Wildlife Waystation, California Photograph by Dave Welling

June

15
monday

16
tuesday

New Moon ●

17
wednesday

18
thursday

19
friday

JUNE

S	M	T	W	T	F	S
	1	2	3	4	5	6
7	8	9	10	11	12	13
14	15	16	17	18	19	20
21	22	23	24	25	26	27
28	29	30				

JULY

S	M	T	W	T	F	S
			1	2	3	4
5	6	7	8	9	10	11
12	13	14	15	16	17	18
19	20	21	22	23	24	25
26	27	28	29	30	31	

20
saturday

21
sunday

Father's Day (U.S., Canada, U.K.) Summer Solstice

June

22
monday

23
tuesday

24
wednesday

First Quarter ◐

25
thursday

26
friday

27
saturday

28
sunday

JUNE

S	M	T	W	T	F	S
	1	2	3	4	5	6
7	8	9	10	11	12	13
14	15	16	17	18	19	20
21	22	23	24	25	26	27
28	29	30				

JULY

S	M	T	W	T	F	S
			1	2	3	4
5	6	7	8	9	10	11
12	13	14	15	16	17	18
19	20	21	22	23	24	25
26	27	28	29	30	31	

In the forest of incarnations I flit gaily from tree to tree.
I shall alight at last, O Lord, upon Thine outstretched hand.

—Paramahansa Yogananda

Summer tanager in cortez amarillo tree, Costa Rica   Photograph by John Hendrickson

More confining than stone walls are the prison bars of habit. You carry this invisible prison with you wherever you go. But you can be free! Determine now to break out of the jail of habits and race for freedom.

—Paramahansa Yogananda

Bald eagle, Alaska Photograph by John Hendrickson

June/July

29
monday

30
tuesday

1
wednesday
Canada Day (Canada) Full Moon ○

2
thursday

3
friday

4
saturday
Independence Day

5
sunday

June

S	M	T	W	T	F	S
	1	2	3	4	5	6
7	8	9	10	11	12	13
14	15	16	17	18	19	20
21	22	23	24	25	26	27
28	29	30				

July

S	M	T	W	T	F	S
			1	2	3	4
5	6	7	8	9	10	11
12	13	14	15	16	17	18
19	20	21	22	23	24	25
26	27	28	29	30	31	

July

6
monday

7
tuesday

8
wednesday

Last Quarter ◑

9
thursday

10
friday

11
saturday

12
sunday

JULY

S	M	T	W	T	F	S
			1	2	3	4
5	6	7	8	9	10	11
12	13	14	15	16	17	18
19	20	21	22	23	24	25
26	27	28	29	30	31	

AUGUST

S	M	T	W	T	F	S
						1
2	3	4	5	6	7	8
9	10	11	12	13	14	15
16	17	18	19	20	21	22
23/30	24/31	25	26	27	28	29

You see only the gross material products coming from God's hidden factory behind creation; but if you went into the factory itself, you would behold in what marvelous manner everything in this world has been brought into manifestation.

—Paramahansa Yogananda

Kilauea lava flow, Kalapana, Hawaii   Photograph by Stuart Westmorland

Deep sincerity is necessary in the spiritual path.
In guilelessness comes the birth of Spirit.

—Paramahansa Yogananda

Black-tail deer fawn, Hurricane Ridge, Washington   Photograph by Ken Archer

July

13
monday

14
tuesday

New Moon ●

15
wednesday

16
thursday

17
friday

JULY

S	M	T	W	T	F	S
			1	2	3	4
5	6	7	8	9	10	11
12	13	14	15	16	17	18
19	20	21	22	23	24	25
26	27	28	29	30	31	

AUGUST

S	M	T	W	T	F	S
						1
2	3	4	5	6	7	8
9	10	11	12	13	14	15
16	17	18	19	20	21	22
23/30	24/31	25	26	27	28	29

18
saturday

19
sunday

20
monday

21
tuesday

22
wednesday

23
thursday
First Quarter ◐

24
friday

25
saturday
Mahavatar Babaji Commemoration Day

26
sunday

JULY

S	M	T	W	T	F	S
			1	2	3	4
5	6	7	8	9	10	11
12	13	14	15	16	17	18
19	20	21	22	23	24	25
26	27	28	29	30	31	

AUGUST

S	M	T	W	T	F	S
						1
2	3	4	5	6	7	8
9	10	11	12	13	14	15
16	17	18	19	20	21	22
23/30	24/31	25	26	27	28	29

Do not leave anybody out of your love.
Keep everyone in your heart, and they will keep you in theirs.

—Paramahansa Yogananda

Eastern tiger swallowtail butterfly, Sammamish, Washington   Photograph by Darrell Gulin

Everything in the phenomenal world displays activity and changefulness, but tranquility is the nature of God.

—Paramahansa Yogananda

Light reflecting on water lilies, France Photograph by Michel Loup/Biosphoto/SteveBloom.com

July/August

27
monday

28
tuesday

29
wednesday

30
thursday

31
friday

Full Moon ◯

JULY

S	M	T	W	T	F	S
			1	2	3	4
5	6	7	8	9	10	11
12	13	14	15	16	17	18
19	20	21	22	23	24	25
26	27	28	29	30	31	

AUGUST

S	M	T	W	T	F	S
						1
2	3	4	5	6	7	8
9	10	11	12	13	14	15
16	17	18	19	20	21	22
23/30	24/31	25	26	27	28	29

1
saturday

2
sunday

August

3
monday
Summer Bank Holiday (Scotland)

4
tuesday

5
wednesday

6
thursday
Last Quarter ◑

7
friday

8
saturday

9
sunday

AUGUST

S	M	T	W	T	F	S
						1
2	3	4	5	6	7	8
9	10	11	12	13	14	15
16	17	18	19	20	21	22
23/30	24/31	25	26	27	28	29

SEPTEMBER

S	M	T	W	T	F	S
		1	2	3	4	5
6	7	8	9	10	11	12
13	14	15	16	17	18	19
20	21	22	23	24	25	26
27	28	29	30			

An unbiased mind is like a clear mirror,
held steady, not oscillating with hasty judgments.

—Paramahansa Yogananda

Sierra Mountains, near Bishop, California   Photograph by Dennis Flaherty

Practice the art of living in this world without losing your inner peace of mind. Follow the path of balance to reach the inner wondrous garden of Self-realization.

—Paramahansa Yogananda

Lotus flower Photograph by SUPERSTOCK

August

10
monday

11
tuesday

12
wednesday

13
thursday

14
friday

New Moon ●

AUGUST

S	M	T	W	T	F	S
						1
2	3	4	5	6	7	8
9	10	11	12	13	14	15
16	17	18	19	20	21	22
23/30	24/31	25	26	27	28	29

SEPTEMBER

S	M	T	W	T	F	S
		1	2	3	4	5
6	7	8	9	10	11	12
13	14	15	16	17	18	19
20	21	22	23	24	25	26
27	28	29	30			

15
saturday

16
sunday

17
monday

18
tuesday

19
wednesday

20
thursday

21
friday

22
saturday

First Quarter ◐

23
sunday

August

S	M	T	W	T	F	S
						1
2	3	4	5	6	7	8
9	10	11	12	13	14	15
16	17	18	19	20	21	22
23/30	24/31	25	26	27	28	29

September

S	M	T	W	T	F	S
		1	2	3	4	5
6	7	8	9	10	11	12
13	14	15	16	17	18	19
20	21	22	23	24	25	26
27	28	29	30			

Peace is everywhere. You are swimming in an ocean of peace.

—Paramahansa Yogananda

Schooling fairy basslets, Fiji Photograph by Stuart Westmorland

Those who meditate feel a wonderful inner quiet....
What you learn in meditation, practice in activity and conversation;
let no one dislodge you from that calm state.

—Paramahansa Yogananda

Salt marsh and Little River, Massachusetts   Photograph by Paul Rezendes

August

24
monday

25
tuesday

26
wednesday

27
thursday

28
friday

AUGUST

S	M	T	W	T	F	S
						1
2	3	4	5	6	7	8
9	10	11	12	13	14	15
16	17	18	19	20	21	22
23/30	24/31	25	26	27	28	29

SEPTEMBER

S	M	T	W	T	F	S
		1	2	3	4	5
6	7	8	9	10	11	12
13	14	15	16	17	18	19
20	21	22	23	24	25	26
27	28	29	30			

Full Moon ○

29
saturday

30
sunday

August/September

31
monday
Summer Bank Holiday (England, Wales & N. Ireland)

1
tuesday

2
wednesday

3
thursday

4
friday

5
saturday
Janmashtami Last Quarter ◑

6
sunday
Father's Day (Australia and N.Z.)

AUGUST

S	M	T	W	T	F	S
						1
2	3	4	5	6	7	8
9	10	11	12	13	14	15
16	17	18	19	20	21	22
23/30	24/31	25	26	27	28	29

SEPTEMBER

S	M	T	W	T	F	S
		1	2	3	4	5
6	7	8	9	10	11	12
13	14	15	16	17	18	19
20	21	22	23	24	25	26
27	28	29	30			

In every atom of this astounding universe,
God is ceaselessly working miracles.

—Paramahansa Yogananda

Luna moth, Sammamish, Washington   Photograph by Darrell Gulin

Everything emerges from the Invisible, to play upon this earth for a little while, and then enters the invisible state again at the end of life.

—Paramahansa Yogananda

Woodland color in autumn fog, Norfolk, United Kingdom Photograph by PHOTOSHOT

September

Labor Day (U.S. and Canada)

7 monday

8 tuesday

9 wednesday

10 thursday

11 friday

September

S	M	T	W	T	F	S
		1	2	3	4	5
6	7	8	9	10	11	12
13	14	15	16	17	18	19
20	21	22	23	24	25	26
27	28	29	30			

October

S	M	T	W	T	F	S
				1	2	3
4	5	6	7	8	9	10
11	12	13	14	15	16	17
18	19	20	21	22	23	24
25	26	27	28	29	30	31

New Moon ●

12 saturday

Rosh Hashanah

13 sunday

14
monday

15
tuesday

16
wednesday

17
thursday

18
friday

19
saturday

20
sunday

September

S	M	T	W	T	F	S
		1	2	3	4	5
6	7	8	9	10	11	12
13	14	15	16	17	18	19
20	21	22	23	24	25	26
27	28	29	30			

October

S	M	T	W	T	F	S
				1	2	3
4	5	6	7	8	9	10
11	12	13	14	15	16	17
18	19	20	21	22	23	24
25	26	27	28	29	30	31

No one else has a personality just like yours.
No one else has a face like yours.
No one else has a soul like yours.
You are a unique creation of God.

—Paramahansa Yogananda

Green sea turtle, near Balicasag Island, Philippines Photograph by Tim Fitzharris

We should bathe our spirits in the deep, pure feeling that stirs within us
when we gaze on the glories of His creation.
This is the way to know God as beauty.

—Paramahansa Yogananda

Saguaro and cholla cactus, Sonoran Desert, Arizona   Photograph by Dennis Frates

September

21
monday

U.N. International Day of Peace   First Quarter ◐

22
tuesday

Yom Kippur

23
wednesday

Autumnal Equinox

24
thursday

25
friday

September

S	M	T	W	T	F	S
		1	2	3	4	5
6	7	8	9	10	11	12
13	14	15	16	17	18	19
20	21	22	23	24	25	26
27	28	29	30			

October

S	M	T	W	T	F	S
				1	2	3
4	5	6	7	8	9	10
11	12	13	14	15	16	17
18	19	20	21	22	23	24
25	26	27	28	29	30	31

26
saturday

Lahiri Mahasaya's Mahasamadhi

27
sunday

Full Moon ○

September/October

28
monday

29
tuesday

30
wednesday

Lahiri Mahasaya's Birthday

1
thursday

2
friday

3
saturday

4
sunday

Last Quarter ◑

SEPTEMBER

S	M	T	W	T	F	S
		1	2	3	4	5
6	7	8	9	10	11	12
13	14	15	16	17	18	19
20	21	22	23	24	25	26
27	28	29	30			

OCTOBER

S	M	T	W	T	F	S
				1	2	3
4	5	6	7	8	9	10
11	12	13	14	15	16	17
18	19	20	21	22	23	24
25	26	27	28	29	30	31

When the mud of your restless thoughts begins to settle,
the power of God begins to reflect in the clear waters of your consciousness.

—Paramahansa Yogananda

North Fork Silver Creek, Silver Falls State Park, Oregon   Photograph by Dennis Frates

Any time you become fascinated by some material creation,
close your eyes, look within, and contemplate its Source.

—Paramahansa Yogananda

Crown jellyfish, Red Sea, Egypt   Photograph by Wolfgang Polzer

October

5
monday

6
tuesday

7
wednesday

8
thursday

9
friday

OCTOBER

S	M	T	W	T	F	S
				1	2	3
4	5	6	7	8	9	10
11	12	13	14	15	16	17
18	19	20	21	22	23	24
25	26	27	28	29	30	31

NOVEMBER

S	M	T	W	T	F	S
1	2	3	4	5	6	7
8	9	10	11	12	13	14
15	16	17	18	19	20	21
22	23	24	25	26	27	28
29	30					

10
saturday

11
sunday

October

12
monday

Columbus Day Thanksgiving Day (Canada) New Moon ●

13
tuesday

14
wednesday

15
thursday

16
friday

17
saturday

18
sunday

October

S	M	T	W	T	F	S
				1	2	3
4	5	6	7	8	9	10
11	12	13	14	15	16	17
18	19	20	21	22	23	24
25	26	27	28	29	30	31

November

S	M	T	W	T	F	S
1	2	3	4	5	6	7
8	9	10	11	12	13	14
15	16	17	18	19	20	21
22	23	24	25	26	27	28
29	30					

Your real nature is calmness....It is time you remember who you are: the blessed soul, a reflection of Spirit.

—Paramahansa Yogananda

Snowdonia, United Kingdom   Photograph by Guy Edwardes

Divine consciousness, with its heavenly bliss, is the subtle alchemist that instantly transmutes the base lead of prosaic mundane life into the radiant gold of unending happiness.

—Paramahansa Yogananda

Early morning light in beech forest, Baden-Wuerttemberg, Germany Photograph by Sailer Images/DRK PHOTO

October

19
monday

20
tuesday
First Quarter ◐

21
wednesday

22
thursday

23
friday

October

S	M	T	W	T	F	S
				1	2	3
4	5	6	7	8	9	10
11	12	13	14	15	16	17
18	19	20	21	22	23	24
25	26	27	28	29	30	31

November

S	M	T	W	T	F	S
1	2	3	4	5	6	7
8	9	10	11	12	13	14
15	16	17	18	19	20	21
22	23	24	25	26	27	28
29	30					

24
saturday

25
sunday
Daylight Saving Time ends (E.U.)

October/November

26
monday
Labour Day (N.Z.)

27
tuesday
Full Moon ○

28
wednesday

29
thursday

30
friday

31
saturday
Halloween (U.S., Canada, U.K.)

1
sunday
Daylight Saving Time ends (U.S. and Canada)

October

S	M	T	W	T	F	S
				1	2	3
4	5	6	7	8	9	10
11	12	13	14	15	16	17
18	19	20	21	22	23	24
25	26	27	28	29	30	31

November

S	M	T	W	T	F	S
1	2	3	4	5	6	7
8	9	10	11	12	13	14
15	16	17	18	19	20	21
22	23	24	25	26	27	28
29	30					

Your

2016 Inner Reflections Engagement Calendar

is now available in bookstores.

You may also place your order directly from Self-Realization Fellowship
by calling 818-549-5151 Monday – Friday from 9:00 a.m. to 5:00 p.m. Pacific time
or order online at:
www.srfbooks.org

If you would like a free copy of Self-Realization Fellowship's complete
catalog of books and recordings, please request it by phone or
fill out the form below and fax or mail it to:

Self-Realization Fellowship
3880 San Rafael Ave.
Los Angeles, CA 90065-3219 U.S.A.
Fax: 800-801-1952

Name: ______________________________

Address: ______________________________

City: ____________________ State: _____ Zip code: __________

Daytime phone: ____________________ Date: ____________________

If you sit night after night practicing meditation and crying to God, the darkness will be burned up, and you will see the Light behind this physical light, the Life behind all life.

—Paramahansa Yogananda

Northern lights and igloo, Manitoba, Canada   Photograph by Steve Bloom/SteveBloom.com

All paths are paths to God,
because, ultimately, there is no other place for the soul to go.

—Paramahansa Yogananda

El Capitan and the Merced River, Yosemite National Park, California Photograph by Mary Liz Austin

November

2
monday

3
tuesday
General Election Day Last Quarter ◑

4
wednesday

5
thursday
Guy Fawkes Day (England)

6
friday

NOVEMBER

S	M	T	W	T	F	S
1	2	3	4	5	6	7
8	9	10	11	12	13	14
15	16	17	18	19	20	21
22	23	24	25	26	27	28
29	30					

DECEMBER

S	M	T	W	T	F	S
		1	2	3	4	5
6	7	8	9	10	11	12
13	14	15	16	17	18	19
20	21	22	23	24	25	26
27	28	29	30	31		

7
saturday

8
sunday
Remembrance Sunday (U.K.)

November

9
monday

10
tuesday

11
wednesday
Veterans Day Remembrance Day (Canada) New Moon ●

12
thursday

13
friday

14
saturday

15
sunday

November

S	M	T	W	T	F	S
1	2	3	4	5	6	7
8	9	10	11	12	13	14
15	16	17	18	19	20	21
22	23	24	25	26	27	28
29	30					

December

S	M	T	W	T	F	S
		1	2	3	4	5
6	7	8	9	10	11	12
13	14	15	16	17	18	19
20	21	22	23	24	25	26
27	28	29	30	31		

Exhale and relax, and feel peace spread everywhere, within and without.
Immerse yourself in that peace.

—Paramahansa Yogananda

Golden panda discus, Wildlife World Zoo and Aquarium, Arizona   Photograph by Alan Patrou

What I am, no one else is. I shall be very proud of my divine individuality.

—Paramahansa Yogananda

Great egret, New Port Richey, Florida   Photograph by Cheryl Arena Molennor

November

16
monday

17
tuesday

First Quarter ◐

18
wednesday

19
thursday

20
friday

November

S	M	T	W	T	F	S
1	2	3	4	5	6	7
8	9	10	11	12	13	14
15	16	17	18	19	20	21
22	23	24	25	26	27	28
29	30					

December

S	M	T	W	T	F	S
		1	2	3	4	5
6	7	8	9	10	11	12
13	14	15	16	17	18	19
20	21	22	23	24	25	26
27	28	29	30	31		

21
saturday

22
sunday

November

23
monday

24
tuesday

25
wednesday

Full Moon ○

26
thursday

Thanksgiving Day

27
friday

28
saturday

29
sunday

November

S	M	T	W	T	F	S
1	2	3	4	5	6	7
8	9	10	11	12	13	14
15	16	17	18	19	20	21
22	23	24	25	26	27	28
29	30					

December

S	M	T	W	T	F	S
		1	2	3	4	5
6	7	8	9	10	11	12
13	14	15	16	17	18	19
20	21	22	23	24	25	26
27	28	29	30	31		

Thanksgiving and praise open in your consciousness the way
for spiritual growth and supply to come to you.
Spirit pushes Itself out into visible manifestation
as soon as a channel is opened through which It can flow.

—Paramahansa Yogananda

Lake Bohinj, Triglav National Park, Slovenia Photograph by Guy Edwardes

Our real self, the soul, is immortal. We exist, and that existence is eternal.
The wave comes to the shore, and then goes back to the sea; it is not lost.
It becomes one with the ocean, or returns again in the form of another wave.

—Paramahansa Yogananda

Wailea, Maui, Hawaii   Photograph by Dennis Frates

November/December

30
monday
St. Andrew's Day (Scotland – Observed)

1
tuesday

2
wednesday
Last Quarter ◑

3
thursday

4
friday

November

S	M	T	W	T	F	S
1	2	3	4	5	6	7
8	9	10	11	12	13	14
15	16	17	18	19	20	21
22	23	24	25	26	27	28
29	30					

5
saturday

December

S	M	T	W	T	F	S
		1	2	3	4	5
6	7	8	9	10	11	12
13	14	15	16	17	18	19
20	21	22	23	24	25	26
27	28	29	30	31		

6
sunday
Hanukkah

December

7
monday

8
tuesday

9
wednesday

10
thursday

11
friday

New Moon ●

12
saturday

13
sunday

December

S	M	T	W	T	F	S
		1	2	3	4	5
6	7	8	9	10	11	12
13	14	15	16	17	18	19
20	21	22	23	24	25	26
27	28	29	30	31		

January 2016

S	M	T	W	T	F	S
					1	2
3	4	5	6	7	8	9
10	11	12	13	14	15	16
17	18	19	20	21	22	23
24/31	25	26	27	28	29	30

On the tract of Eternity, I built an unseen church where all might worship. Here, under the blue dome, illumined by sun, moon, aurora, milky way, and wisdom lights, are gathered the assembled star families, island universes, solar systems, and the little earth with its millions of votaries of many religions.

—Paramahansa Yogananda

Lake Bled, Julian Alps, Slovenia   Photograph by Guy Edwardes

*O*ut of the changeful waters of life, let us salvage through meditation
the diamond of unchangeable soul-consciousness,
which sparkles with the everlasting joy of Spirit.

—Paramahansa Yogananda

Ice covered branches, Jura region, France Photograph by Michel Loup/Biosphoto/SteveBloom.com

December

14
monday

15
tuesday

16
wednesday

17
thursday

18
friday

First Quarter ◐

December

S	M	T	W	T	F	S
		1	2	3	4	5
6	7	8	9	10	11	12
13	14	15	16	17	18	19
20	21	22	23	24	25	26
27	28	29	30	31		

January 2016

S	M	T	W	T	F	S
					1	2
3	4	5	6	7	8	9
10	11	12	13	14	15	16
17	18	19	20	21	22	23
24/31	25	26	27	28	29	30

19
saturday

20
sunday

December

21
monday
Winter Solstice

22
tuesday

23
wednesday

24
thursday

25
friday
Christmas Full Moon ◯

26
saturday
Boxing Day (Canada)

27
sunday

December

S	M	T	W	T	F	S
		1	2	3	4	5
6	7	8	9	10	11	12
13	14	15	16	17	18	19
20	21	22	23	24	25	26
27	28	29	30	31		

January 2016

S	M	T	W	T	F	S
					1	2
3	4	5	6	7	8	9
10	11	12	13	14	15	16
17	18	19	20	21	22	23
24/31	25	26	27	28	29	30

The love that dwells in the souls of all creatures—
the sum and perfection of the love of all mothers, all fathers, all friends, all lovers—
that is Christ-love.

—Paramahansa Yogananda

Robin, seen through frost, Bedfordshire, United Kingdom Photograph by Brian Bevan/Ardea/Animals Animals

Make me realize that with the dawn of Thy light,
the darkness will vanish
as though it had never been.

—Paramahansa Yogananda

River Avon, Worchestershire, United Kingdom   Photograph by nagelstock.com/Alamy

December/January

28
monday

Boxing Day (U.K., Australia, N.Z. – Observed)

29
tuesday

30
wednesday

31
thursday

1
friday

New Year's Day Last Quarter ◑

2
saturday

3
sunday

DECEMBER

S	M	T	W	T	F	S
		1	2	3	4	5
6	7	8	9	10	11	12
13	14	15	16	17	18	19
20	21	22	23	24	25	26
27	28	29	30	31		

JANUARY 2016

S	M	T	W	T	F	S
					1	2
3	4	5	6	7	8	9
10	11	12	13	14	15	16
17	18	19	20	21	22	23
24/31	25	26	27	28	29	30

NOTES

ACKNOWLEDGMENTS

We wish to express our sincere appreciation to the following photographers and agencies who contributed to this year's *Inner Reflections* engagement calendar. Following a contributor's name, in parentheses, is the month and a day of the week, or other description, where each photo appears.

Alamy (6/1; 12/28)

Animals Animals (1/12; 5/25; 12/21)

Ken Archer (7/13)

Ardea (5/25; 12/21)

Mary Liz Austin (11/2)

Brian Bevan (12/21)

Biosphoto (7/27; 12/14)

Steve Bloom/SteveBloom.com (3/23; 7/27; 10/26; 12/14)

Phyllis Burchett (4/6; 4/20)

Russ Burden (2/16)

Marie Bush (4/27)

CCOphotostockKMN (1/19)

Jon Cornforth (5/18)

Terry Donnelly (cover)

DRK Images (10/19)

Guy Edwardes (3/30; 6/8; 10/12; 11/23; 12/7)

Tim Fitzharris (2/2; 9/14)

Dennis Flaherty (8/3)

Dennis Frates (1/26; 3/2; 3/16; 9/21; 9/28; 11/30)

Getty Images (3/30)

Daisy Gilardini (2/23)

Darrell Gulin (3/9; 7/20; 8/31)

John Hendrickson (6/22; 6/29)

Jaynes' Gallery/Danita Delimont Agency (5/11)

Gerard Lacz (1/12)

Michel Loup (7/27; 12/14)

Masterfile (2/23)

Kevin McNeil (4/13)

Cheryl Arena Molennor (5/4; 11/16)

Nagelstock.com (12/28)

Jay O'Brien (5/11)

Marion Owen (1/5)

Alan Patrou (11/9)

PHOTOSHOT (9/7)

Wolfgang Polzer (10/5)

Prisma (1/19)

Paul Rezendes (12/29/14; 8/24)

Sailer Images (10/19)

David Speight (6/1)

Steffen & Alexandra (5/25)

SUPERSTOCK (1/19; 8/10)

Steve Terrill (2/9)

Dave Welling (6/15)

Stuart Westmorland (7/6; 8/17)

About Paramahansa Yogananda

Paramahansa Yogananda
1893-1952

All the quotes featured in *Inner Reflections* have been selected from the writings of Paramahansa Yogananda, one of the preeminent spiritual teachers of the 20th century. Yogananda came to the United States in 1920 as India's delegate to an international congress of religious leaders convening in Boston. He remained in the West for the better part of the next thirty-two years, conducting classes in cities across America, counseling, and creating a monumental body of written work.

Paramahansa Yogananda's life story, *Autobiography of a Yogi,* is considered a modern spiritual classic. It was selected one of "The Top 100 Spiritual Books of the Twentieth Century" in a survey conducted by HarperCollins. A perennial best seller since it was first published in 1946, *Autobiography of a Yogi* has been translated into more than thirty languages and is widely used in college and university courses.

For more information about SRF publications and the teachings of Paramahansa Yogananda, please visit our website:

www.yogananda-srf.org

Self-Realization Fellowship
FOUNDED 1920 BY PARAMAHANSA YOGANANDA

SELF-REALIZATION FELLOWSHIP, the international nonprofit society founded by Paramahansa Yogananda, is dedicated to carrying on his spiritual and humanitarian work — fostering a spirit of greater harmony and understanding among those of all nations and faiths, and introducing truth-seekers around the world to his universal teachings on the ancient science of Yoga.

A SELECTION OF BOOKS BY PARAMAHANSA YOGANANDA

Available at bookstores or from our website:
www.srfbooks.org

Autobiography of a Yogi

Autobiography of a Yogi *(Audiobook, read by Sir Ben Kingsley)*

The Science of Religion

The Law of Success

How You Can Talk With God

Metaphysical Meditations

Where There Is Light: *Insight and Inspiration for Meeting Life's Challenges*

The Yoga of Jesus: *Understanding the Hidden Teachings of the Gospels*

The Yoga of the Bhagavad Gita: *An Introduction to India's Universal Science of God-Realization*

THE COLLECTED TALKS AND ESSAYS

Volume I: Man's Eternal Quest

Volume II: The Divine Romance

Volume III: Journey to Self-realization

SELF-REALIZATION FELLOWSHIP LESSONS

The scientific techniques of meditation taught by Paramahansa Yogananda, including *Kriya Yoga* — as well as his guidance on all aspects of balanced spiritual living — are taught in the *Self-Realization Fellowship Lessons.* For further information, we welcome you to request the free booklet *Undreamed-of Possibilities.*

SELF-REALIZATION FELLOWSHIP

3880 San Rafael Avenue • Los Angeles, CA 90065-3219

TEL (323) 225-2471 • FAX (323) 225-5088

www.yogananda-srf.org

2014

January

s	m	t	w	t	f	s
			1	2	3	4
5	6	7	8	9	10	11
12	13	14	15	16	17	18
19	20	21	22	23	24	25
26	27	28	29	30	31	

February

s	m	t	w	t	f	s
						1
2	3	4	5	6	7	8
9	10	11	12	13	14	15
16	17	18	19	20	21	22
23	24	25	26	27	28	

March

s	m	t	w	t	f	s
						1
2	3	4	5	6	7	8
9	10	11	12	13	14	15
16	17	18	19	20	21	22
23/30	24/31	25	26	27	28	29

April

s	m	t	w	t	f	s
		1	2	3	4	5
6	7	8	9	10	11	12
13	14	15	16	17	18	19
20	21	22	23	24	25	26
27	28	29	30			

May

s	m	t	w	t	f	s
				1	2	3
4	5	6	7	8	9	10
11	12	13	14	15	16	17
18	19	20	21	22	23	24
25	26	27	28	29	30	31

June

s	m	t	w	t	f	s
1	2	3	4	5	6	7
8	9	10	11	12	13	14
15	16	17	18	19	20	21
22	23	24	25	26	27	28
29	30					

July

s	m	t	w	t	f	s
		1	2	3	4	5
6	7	8	9	10	11	12
13	14	15	16	17	18	19
20	21	22	23	24	25	26
27	28	29	30	31		

August

s	m	t	w	t	f	s
					1	2
3	4	5	6	7	8	9
10	11	12	13	14	15	16
17	18	19	20	21	22	23
24/31	25	26	27	28	29	30

September

s	m	t	w	t	f	s
	1	2	3	4	5	6
7	8	9	10	11	12	13
14	15	16	17	18	19	20
21	22	23	24	25	26	27
28	29	30				

October

s	m	t	w	t	f	s
			1	2	3	4
5	6	7	8	9	10	11
12	13	14	15	16	17	18
19	20	21	22	23	24	25
26	27	28	29	30	31	

November

s	m	t	w	t	f	s
						1
2	3	4	5	6	7	8
9	10	11	12	13	14	15
16	17	18	19	20	21	22
23/30	24	25	26	27	28	29

December

s	m	t	w	t	f	s
	1	2	3	4	5	6
7	8	9	10	11	12	13
14	15	16	17	18	19	20
21	22	23	24	25	26	27
28	29	30	31			

2016

January

s	m	t	w	t	f	s
					1	2
3	4	5	6	7	8	9
10	11	12	13	14	15	16
17	18	19	20	21	22	23
24/31	25	26	27	28	29	30

February

s	m	t	w	t	f	s
	1	2	3	4	5	6
7	8	9	10	11	12	13
14	15	16	17	18	19	20
21	22	23	24	25	26	27
28	29					

March

s	m	t	w	t	f	s
		1	2	3	4	5
6	7	8	9	10	11	12
13	14	15	16	17	18	19
20	21	22	23	24	25	26
27	28	29	30	31		

April

s	m	t	w	t	f	s
					1	2
3	4	5	6	7	8	9
10	11	12	13	14	15	16
17	18	19	20	21	22	23
24	25	26	27	28	29	30

May

s	m	t	w	t	f	s
1	2	3	4	5	6	7
8	9	10	11	12	13	14
15	16	17	18	19	20	21
22	23	24	25	26	27	28
29	30	31				

June

s	m	t	w	t	f	s
			1	2	3	4
5	6	7	8	9	10	11
12	13	14	15	16	17	18
19	20	21	22	23	24	25
26	27	28	29	30		

July

s	m	t	w	t	f	s
					1	2
3	4	5	6	7	8	9
10	11	12	13	14	15	16
17	18	19	20	21	22	23
24/31	25	26	27	28	29	30

August

s	m	t	w	t	f	s
	1	2	3	4	5	6
7	8	9	10	11	12	13
14	15	16	17	18	19	20
21	22	23	24	25	26	27
28	29	30	31			

September

s	m	t	w	t	f	s
				1	2	3
4	5	6	7	8	9	10
11	12	13	14	15	16	17
18	19	20	21	22	23	24
25	26	27	28	29	30	

October

s	m	t	w	t	f	s
						1
2	3	4	5	6	7	8
9	10	11	12	13	14	15
16	17	18	19	20	21	22
23/30	24/31	25	26	27	28	29

November

s	m	t	w	t	f	s
		1	2	3	4	5
6	7	8	9	10	11	12
13	14	15	16	17	18	19
20	21	22	23	24	25	26
27	28	29	30			

December

s	m	t	w	t	f	s
				1	2	3
4	5	6	7	8	9	10
11	12	13	14	15	16	17
18	19	20	21	22	23	24
25	26	27	28	29	30	31

2015

January

s	m	t	w	t	f	s
				1	2	3
4	5	6	7	8	9	10
11	12	13	14	15	16	17
18	19	20	21	22	23	24
25	26	27	28	29	30	31

February

s	m	t	w	t	f	s
1	2	3	4	5	6	7
8	9	10	11	12	13	14
15	16	17	18	19	20	21
22	23	24	25	26	27	28

March

s	m	t	w	t	f	s
1	2	3	4	5	6	7
8	9	10	11	12	13	14
15	16	17	18	19	20	21
22	23	24	25	26	27	28
29	30	31				

April

s	m	t	w	t	f	s
			1	2	3	4
5	6	7	8	9	10	11
12	13	14	15	16	17	18
19	20	21	22	23	24	25
26	27	28	29	30		

May

s	m	t	w	t	f	s
					1	2
3	4	5	6	7	8	9
10	11	12	13	14	15	16
17	18	19	20	21	22	23
24/31	25	26	27	28	29	30

June

s	m	t	w	t	f	s
	1	2	3	4	5	6
7	8	9	10	11	12	13
14	15	16	17	18	19	20
21	22	23	24	25	26	27
28	29	30				

July

s	m	t	w	t	f	s
			1	2	3	4
5	6	7	8	9	10	11
12	13	14	15	16	17	18
19	20	21	22	23	24	25
26	27	28	29	30	31	

August

s	m	t	w	t	f	s
						1
2	3	4	5	6	7	8
9	10	11	12	13	14	15
16	17	18	19	20	21	22
23/30	24/31	25	26	27	28	29

September

s	m	t	w	t	f	s
		1	2	3	4	5
6	7	8	9	10	11	12
13	14	15	16	17	18	19
20	21	22	23	24	25	26
27	28	29	30			

October

s	m	t	w	t	f	s
				1	2	3
4	5	6	7	8	9	10
11	12	13	14	15	16	17
18	19	20	21	22	23	24
25	26	27	28	29	30	31

November

s	m	t	w	t	f	s
1	2	3	4	5	6	7
8	9	10	11	12	13	14
15	16	17	18	19	20	21
22	23	24	25	26	27	28
29	30					

December

s	m	t	w	t	f	s
		1	2	3	4	5
6	7	8	9	10	11	12
13	14	15	16	17	18	19
20	21	22	23	24	25	26
27	28	29	30	31		

January

Sunday	Monday	Tuesday	Wednesday	Thursday	Friday	Saturday
				1	2	3
4	5	6	7	8	9	10
11	12	13	14	15	16	17
18	19	20	21	22	23	24
25	26	27	28	29	30	31

Jan 1 New Year's Day
Jan 2 Bank Holiday (U.K.)
Day After New Year's Day (N.Z.)
Jan 5 Paramahansa Yogananda's Birthday
Jan 19 Martin Luther King, Jr.'s Birthday (Observed)
Jan 26 Australia Day (Australia)

February

Sunday	Monday	Tuesday	Wednesday	Thursday	Friday	Saturday
1	2	3	4	5	6	7
8	9	10	11	12	13	14
15	16	17	18	19	20	21
22	23	24	25	26	27	28

Feb 6 Waitangi Day (N.Z.)
Feb 12 Lincoln's Birthday
Feb 14 St. Valentine's Day
Feb 16 Presidents' Day
Feb 22 Washington's Birthday

March

Sunday	Monday	Tuesday	Wednesday	Thursday	Friday	Saturday
1	2	3	4	5	6	7
8	9	10	11	12	13	14
15	16	17	18	19	20	21
22	23	24	25	26	27	28
29	30	31				

Mar 1 St. David's Day (Wales)
Mar 7 Paramahansa Yogananda's Mahasamadhi
Mar 8 Daylight Saving Time begins (U.S. and Canada)
Mar 9 Sri Yukteswar's Mahasamadhi
Mar 15 Mothering Sunday (U.K.)
Mar 17 St. Patrick's Day
Mar 20 Vernal Equinox
Mar 29 Daylight Savings Time begins (E.U.)

April

Sunday	Monday	Tuesday	Wednesday	Thursday	Friday	Saturday
			1	2	3	4
5	6	7	8	9	10	11
12	13	14	15	16	17	18
19	20	21	22	23	24	25
26	27	28	29	30		

Apr 3 Passover begins
Good Friday

Apr 5 Easter Sunday

Apr 6 Easter Monday (Canada, U.K., Australia, N.Z.)

Apr 22 Earth Day

Apr 23 St. George's Day (England)

Apr 25 ANZAC Day (Australia and N.Z.)

May

Sunday	Monday	Tuesday	Wednesday	Thursday	Friday	Saturday
					1	2
3	4	5	6	7	8	9
10	11	12	13	14	15	16
17	18	19	20	21	22	23
24	25	26	27	28	29	30
31						

May 4 Early May Bank Holiday (U.K.)

May 7 National Day of Prayer

May 10 Sri Yukteswar's Birthday
Mother's Day (U.S., Canada, Australia, N.Z.)

May 18 Victoria Day (Canada)

May 25 Memorial Day
Spring Bank Holiday (U.K.)

JUNE

Sunday	Monday	Tuesday	Wednesday	Thursday	Friday	Saturday
	1	2	3	4	5	6
7	8	9	10	11	12	13
14	15	16	17	18	19	20
21	22	23	24	25	26	27
28	29	30				

Jun 1	Queen's Birthday (N.Z.)
Jun 8	Queen's Birthday (Australia)
Jun 21	Father's Day (U.S., Canada, U.K.) Summer Solstice

July

Sunday	Monday	Tuesday	Wednesday	Thursday	Friday	Saturday
			1	2	3	4
5	6	7	8	9	10	11
12	13	14	15	16	17	18
19	20	21	22	23	24	25
26	27	28	29	30	31	

Jul 1 Canada Day (Canada)
Jul 4 Independence Day
Jul 25 Mahavatar Babaji Commemoration Day

August

Sunday	Monday	Tuesday	Wednesday	Thursday	Friday	Saturday
						1
2	3	4	5	6	7	8
9	10	11	12	13	14	15
16	17	18	19	20	21	22
23	24	25	26	27	28	29
30	31					

Aug 3 Summer Bank Holiday (Scotland)
Aug 31 Summer Bank Holiday (England, Wales & N. Iteland)

September

Sunday	Monday	Tuesday	Wednesday	Thursday	Friday	Saturday
		1	2	3	4	5
6	7	8	9	10	11	12
13	14	15	16	17	18	19
20	21	22	23	24	25	26
27	28	29	30			

Sep 5 Janmashtami
Sep 6 Father's Day (Australia and N.Z.)
Sep 7 Labor Day (U.S. and Canada)
Sep 13 Rosh Hashanah
Sep 21 U.N. International Day of Peace
Sep 22 Yom Kippur
Sep 23 Autumnal Equinox
Sep 26 Lahiri Mahasaya's Mahasamadhi
Sep 30 Lahiri Mahasaya's Birthday

October

Sunday	Monday	Tuesday	Wednesday	Thursday	Friday	Saturday
				1	2	3
4	5	6	7	8	9	10
11	12	13	14	15	16	17
18	19	20	21	22	23	24
25	26	27	28	29	30	31

Oct 12 Columbus Day
Thanksgiving Day (Canada)
Oct 25 Daylight Saving Time ends (E.U.)

Oct 26 Labour Day (N.Z.)
Oct 31 Halloween (U.S., Canada, U.K.)

November

Sunday	Monday	Tuesday	Wednesday	Thursday	Friday	Saturday
1	2	3	4	5	6	7
8	9	10	11	12	13	14
15	16	17	18	19	20	21
22	23	24	25	26	27	28
29	30					

Nov 1 Daylight Saving Time ends (U.S. and Canada)
Nov 3 General Election Day
Nov 5 Guy Fawkes Day (England)
Nov 8 Remembrance Sunday (U.K.)
Nov 11 Veterans Day
Remembrance Day (Canada)
Nov 26 Thanksgiving Day
Nov 30 St. Andrew's Day (Scotland – Observed)

December

Sunday	Monday	Tuesday	Wednesday	Thursday	Friday	Saturday
		1	2	3	4	5
6	7	8	9	10	11	12
13	14	15	16	17	18	19
20	21	22	23	24	25	26
27	28	29	30	31		

Dec 6 Hanukkah
Dec 21 Winter Solstice
Dec 25 Christmas
Dec 26 Boxing Day (Canada)
Dec 28 Boxing Day (U.K., Australia, N.Z.)

NOTES